You Are A WONDER

FOREWARD
By the Author

I was never a poet but I always loved to create and tell
stories. It was only the past few years that I started to
speak and write poetic rhymes that have a spark of
inspiration, a story and also gave food for the soul. I
would write and post these poems on social media to help
my friends and strangers alike, who would later comment
and tell me how it helped them that morning, or that my
posts would remind them to stay in their centre during
some hard and trying times, especially when everything
in society has many forms of distractions that pull us
away from our centre.

I dedicate this book to all those who need a little light
along the path of a darkening world and I hope these
rhymes and sayings will keep you on your inward journey
– some to remind you who You truly are, some to put a
smile on your face and perhaps some, to make you
question things.

With the deepest respect to your life and journey...

Your Spirit Brother,
Steven Benitez

TITLES

TRUST

Trust your path,
Trust the light within you,
It may be a little lonely,
Into the unknown where things
are not greatly clear.
But I would like to whisper to you today,
"Your light is always shining!"
It's there beyond the fears,
Beyond the past emotions,
Beyond the hurts,
Beyond the disappointments,
Beyond the pain,
Your light is always shining.
Once you sit,
Let go,
Relax a little,
It will surface by itself.
It was always there, because it is you.
It's your real eyes,
It's your real ears,

It's your awareness,
And your greatest treasure.
You are priceless.
Beyond comprehension.
Beyond anything money can buy.
That is you!"

SPACE

The space to recover, to think,
When this world moves faster than a blink.
Space to inhale and exhale
when you're feeling frail.
The space to be weak,
and to be called a freak.
The space to allow yourself to
make some mistakes.
The space to forgive yourself
when your feet miss the brakes.
Space to wonder and create as you feel.
The space to allow yourself to be totally real.
The space to discover at your free will.
The space to choose,
and express your different views.
The space to talk and walk freely.
To choose to be or not to be.
That is still the question.

YOUR SACRED HEART

You see that precious part
we call the heart?
That thing that beats about 115,000
times each day.
Pumping an average of 2,000 gallons
of vital fluid?
It's beating,
It's keeping you in this very meeting.
It's a proven fact that your heart
likes to laugh.
It loves to sing,
It enjoys a smile,
It wants to love,
to share and care.
But that will only happen if you dare.
Stress free,
Without a worry.
So let your hearts be merry.
From this centre,
Your mouth speaks,

Your thoughts flow,
You sense,
You create,
You see the invisible,
and make it visible.
There's a beautiful saying,
It reads:
"Blessed are the pure in heart,
for they shall see God."
The highest reward,
to see the All in all.
The light of light,
In trees,
In you and me.
A face to face,
No more need to chase.
The search is over,
When the heart is kept pure,
The ultimate cure,
In this I am sure.
The heart and brain
are in constant communication,

Like two lovers,
Sending information,
for every situation.
So when you listen to its sound,
The waves,
The motion,
You'll soon discover
it's like a vast ocean
of wild devotion.
This chamber,
This place of dwelling,
This secret place,
The sacred space,
It too needs your embrace.

LOVE and SCIENCE

Love and science working together.
Everywhere I go,
I hear the same mantra,
The same rap, but is it a trap?
"Trust the science, it's the only appliance!"
What about trusting your own discernment?
Your own ability to take the responsibility
to rightly see reality.
Trusting the peace in your heart to navigate
and precisely allocate.
You've heard of the Monarch
butterfly's migration,
How this little creature can fly across
vast regions,
Traveling between 50 to 100 miles per day,
And you say, "no way!"
For up to two months,
Without any data or navigation tool,
This little creature is no fool!
"Trust the science!"

Nuclear power - a very potent source,
environmentally friendly or deadly?
You decide! Or are you not qualified?!
Let's ask Chernobyl or Fukushima.
Consider yourself lucky
you weren't living near her.
And what about plastic?
The semi-synthetic materials that were
also put in cheap cereals.
Causing constant harm to our precious
neighbours,
Slowly dying but we continue buying.
And what about the scientific breakthrough of
DDT, short for Dichlorodiphenyltrichloroethane,
A crystalline chemical compound
that was supposed to be safe and sound.
Used to kill mosquitoes,
But the problem they soon discovered,
Is that it killed everything,
From bird, to deer and anything near.
Cancer forming with very little informing!
So go ahead and trust the data,

You still think it's much greater.
What about the virus and bacteria research?
Well, if you follow the cash,
You might find some more trash!
Cold War bio-weapons of mass destruction,
Specifically designed to wipe out every kind.
The political alliance working alongside science.
But trust the scientific historical integrity,
Especially when it's designed to bring them
more prosperity.
Trust the pharmaceutical companies
and their bribes,
They're no different to the religious scribes,
Corroding good science with their wicked vibes.
What about particle physics and its risks?
Genetic engineering and its true purpose,
this is no different than a circus!
Genetically edited babies so that they can
look like a Mercedes!
And gain of function mutation - how do you
know there wasn't a leak?
Don't say that you're a freak!

In a lab, now and you want me to have a jab?
Or has it all gone too far in its operation,
And we are now in a situation,
With too much misinformation.
Cloning humans, synthetic biology, is this really
close to our ecology?
And how will it affect our natural psychology?
What's the real motive?
What's the real intention?
Or is it too late to mention?
"Oh, but one can trust these great finds,
For they are the one with the great minds."
"Trust the data!"
Maybe you can understand why I have no
peace about the whole Corona,
It's like a drama in Pamplona!
There's no release to put a jab
That's come out of your lab!
Science should be a service of love,
In fact, in its pure essence,
it's divine, majestic, creative,
A true gift like a beautiful rift.

But it has to flow with the existing laws
as a service to all life.
In union with the Law of Vibration,
So that it benefits the entire population.
If it co-works with the Law of Causation,
this law will reveal the exact information
and the precise application!
Scientific breakthroughs need to be presented
before wise and fair councils, Discussions and
their repercussions.
So, I conclude and never to be rude,
If science works with the force of Love,
It will find solutions for our current pollution.
So, I will trust the science of Love,
With honesty, as its policy!

WITHOUT INTERFERENCE

Allowing things to be as they are,
From here to afar.
That which is there,
So beautiful and fair.
That which is happening
of its own accord,
If left alone,
Will bring its natural reward.
The "It" breathes you,
The life that lives,
The force that moves,
The Tao that sings,
The light that shines,
Are all its signs.
When we leave things alone,
When we allow space to be,
Nature returns,
We all must learn.

FAITH

"Now faith is the substance of things hoped
for, the evidence of things not seen".
There's a beautiful reason why you see the
world the way your eyes see it, or the way
your heart wants to express itself.
This is what makes you, you!
That's your gift.
It's beautiful, sacred, special, unique, authentic.
It's not for it to be necessarily liked, received,
or even accepted.
In fact, the majority these days will probably
disagree with you on nearly everything!
Data has replaced heart, soul, art,
expression, imagination, magic.
To be honest, it's totally boring.
So let your heart breathe again and live
without fear of what others might think
or not think of you.
Your eyes, your lens, was designed for you to
paint your pictures, to express your heart,

to play your music, to write your chapters,
to leave your magical prints.
This is your sacred call,
it's your sacred moment,
in this part of history.
So have the courage to walk the things you see
and feel are right for you.
The whispers of your heart are there
if you listen.
They may confront all your fears in the
process, but in the end, you will look back and
say, "what a journey!"

YOU ARE LIGHT

You are the light of this world!
You are the light,
Yes you!
Just in case you say,
"Me? Oh no, not me. I am just a little flee,
hiding behind a tree."
You are the lamp that can shine
in any darkness,
That can heat any cold,
That can warm any heart,
That can point to the way,
That can help any stray.
You are the candle that sits on a table,
That can join two hearts
that have fallen apart,
That can sit in a home,
Flickering its magic,
Dissolving the tragic.
You are the torch
that leads the way,

Protecting those falling,
The lost, at all cost.
Are you hearing its calling?
When you shine your light,
You shine your life,
Your love emanates,
It penetrates,
And recreates,
Hope and healing.
The lost get found,
Like your keys on the ground.
You are the light house
that directs the ships,
From wild storms,
Protecting lives,
From unseen waves,
And dangerous caves.
If you only knew its meaning,
Your life would soon be beaming.
You are the light of this world,
So don't lower your worth,
Or sell it over for a purse,

This only leads to a curse!
Your light is your essence,
Your most majestic presence.
It is the real you.
So shine,
Now is your time!
And let out your power,
Without fear,
Be your true self.
Don't hang it on the shelf,
Don't waste it,
Or paste it on the wrong wall.
Please hear my call,
Stand tall,
You are a light,
Deep down you're bright.
Don't let this world
prevent you from shining.
This is your moment,
Your experience.
So immerse,
Go deeper,

Climb steeper.
Your light is your real home.
You are not a clone!
A light always reveals the way,
It opens the path,
And gives direction,
Much more than just a projection.
Light is a sign of life,
An indication that you are alive,
That you have energy,
That your batteries are on,
That your life is moving.
So the question arises:
How does one keep this shining?
The sun flower reveals the key
for you and me.
Observe what it follows,
Today and tomorrow!
Observe its line,
How it sits with its spine.
Observe its alignment,
Its concentration,

Its focus,
Its attention,
With zero tension.
It's only mission,
Its absolute vision,
Is to follow the light of the Sun.

CREATIVE THOUGHTS

Creative ideas are always so very near.
The power to go within,
To paint,
To sketch,
To envision, is your decision.
This is truly one of your many qualities,
Ask Socrates!
Your ability to see with new eyes,
Is the state with no compromise.
The way you see,
And how you see,
It's your very essence expressing
your life with a dressing,
A true blessing.
Let your dreams flow again,
Like living streams.

SPIRIT OF A WOMAN

A spirit of the female warrior,
A woman's strength,
A woman's power,
Her inner quality,
Her true armour,
Her force is of course,
Her power to love.
For love covers
like an ever-increasing tower
Love protects and shields,
And is always ready
to enter the battle fields.
Love forgives,
It lets go,
Always finding the ultimate flow.
Love allows one to breathe,
Giving space and equality
as its foundation policy.
Love perseveres,
It endures to the end,

And is always able to turn a bend.
It's patient and kind
and soothing to your mind.
A small still voice
gently making the right choice.
The Warrior Spirit of a woman is here to stay
and also help all to find their way.

IT BREATHES YOU

It's breathing you,
It's giving you, life.
And it's all happening by itself.
When we stop interfering,
Your true life starts appearing.
Tomorrow is a new day and it's waiting
for you to live it wholeheartedly.

TOTAL SURRENDER

Be the leaf flowing down the stream,
With no interference,
Total surrender,
It finds its splendour.
The deep let go,
Immersed in flow...
Unwavering in its direction,
With a very clear objection,
The leaf forms a union.
With no separation,
It finds its meditation.

MOMENT OF FREEDOM

When you arrive at the place
of accepting, the things you cannot change,
This is your moment of freedom.
Allowing things to rise and fall.
This is your sacred moment.
The energy flows,
And you are free.
To not interfere is to overcome all your fears.
Then all will return to its rightful place,
The sacred space.

WINDOW OF OPPORTUNITY

A new road or path presents itself,
And you have walked this far?
It's been long and weary,
At times even teary.
So you pause, reflect, quick check.
Do I walk through the unknown?
Or will I get blown?
Do I even have the reserves
to climb up those curves?
Or shall I stay, where it's safe.
Have I even got the faith?
But deep down in the pit of your gut
you know you have the strut.
It's time to take that step,
A new stride,
And rise above the tide.
It's calling,
So don't be afraid of falling.
It's honestly an opportunity,
Your chance to dance.

A small step and you can advance.
In this world of unknown mystery,
You can write a new page of your history.
What has appeared has now become
very near.
Your moment has arrived
and you have always survived.

FLOW

The flow of your life,
There's no need for strife.
The gentle currents of truth
moment by moment.
The small still voice, it's really your choice.
No need to fear, for it will steer.
Allowing the Now to flow
will lead the Tao to show.
Open your hearts,
and allow truth to rise,
For this is truly wise.
Moment by moment,
The gentle breeze
will lead with ease.

YOUR INNER STRENGTH

A new disease, a virus,
A crisis, remember Isis?
Everything that rises falls!
Wearing a mask,
I am sure you have been asked.
Social distancing, keep listening,
Potential economic collapse,
More traps, perhaps?!
Explosions, wild emotions,
The rising of the oceans,
Political uncertainty with social unrest,
A time of much confusion,
With many souls suffering in seclusion.
Hear my heart,
There's no need to fall apart.
Wherever there's a will there's a way.
You are more than a conqueror,
Yes, it's a time of change,
But you have to find your new range.
Yes, it's a time of distrust,

But you have to find a new thrust,
No need to go bust!
It's time to visit a new dimension,
To expand internally,
To see a new vision,
Dream a new dream.
To open the windows of the realm of
imagination,
To paint a new picture,
To sing a new song,
Not to shrink,
Or over think!
But instead expand your inner dimensions.
Apply Faith, the substance of things hope for,
To surge with a new spirit,
To raise a new standard,
To call forth your dreams!
This is not a time to quit,
Or fall into a pit.
I am calling you to rise,
To apply the wise,
To move forward,

To dream again,
To see with new eyes,
And have faith in who you are.
Keep moving forward!

YOUR GARDEN IS BEAUTIFUL TOO

One of the biggest blockages you'll have in
your life is to compare yourself with the
progression of others.
Your life and your journey is totally
unique to you.
Your progression is wonderfully timed by your
own unique rhythm and pace.
Everyone is different.
Comparing yourself to others is only a
distraction to you.
Trust your visions, trust your insights,
But allow them to blossom in their own time.
Your garden will form in its own
unique way and time.
Embrace it, enjoy it, become one with it.

PASSING THROUGH

Everything changes,
Moment by moment,
A realistic component.
The law of impermanence,
With nothing to grab
Or nothing to hold,
Not even a cold.
The changes come,
Some not always fun,
In a sudden,
Or over time,
It's a guarantee
for you and me.
Life changes,
It moves with its grooves,
Imparts new moves.
Be ready with new shoes
to hear the expressing blues!
So should one grip,
Hold and clutch?

When everything around us
is changing so much?
With this in mind,
Isn't it better to be more kind?
To walk with an open heart,
Gently, allowing life to flow,
Trusting its show,
Its signs,
Its times,
Its forms,
The shapes,
The patterns,
The seasons
all come and go,
Gently whispering,
"Will you enter my flow?"
So let go
of the trying to control,
Listen to its vision,
To its moving,
And motion,
It's gentle notion,

It's ways,
The invisible rays,
The ever-changing days.
It's here to stay.

LIGHT

Remember you are light, and your light has the
power to overcome any obstacle you are
facing. Your light has the power to brighten
your day or anyone else's day that it touches.
Your light is like the Sun shining through the
heavy clouds. Remember it's light that gives
life, and light that brings clarity.
The absence of your light is the inability to let
your love, joy, and truth express itself.
Darkness is only light, sleeping.
So, it's time to truly wake up and let your light
shine. Just because your shine is different, it
doesn't mean it's wrong. I say stand up and
shine, stand up and let your fragrance come
forth, stand up in the midst of the unrest and
be the rest you feel and see.
Stand up in the midst of lack and be the cup
that is overflowing with goodness and mercy.
Stand up with all the other lights shining and
know that our corporate light has enough

power to cause a revival, a renewal, a great change, a real awakening and not a fake reset. We are not machines that have a reset button. We are spirit and light, called to shine bright!

THE LOTUS KEMBANGAN

Through the sticky, hard dense mud it rises.
The struggle, the pain,
It can feel almost in vain.
But it rises,
Beautifully surprising.
Soft and gentle,
Trusting it's centre amidst the madness,
The deep sadness,
with an appealing gladness.
The Lotus Kembangan,
The soft flow,
It's not for show.
The all-encompassing dance
That leads you to the correct trance.
The interweaving gestures
And postures it fosters,
In the end it prospers!
Finding union,
Erasing the confusion,
The deep delusions,

Eliminating pollution.
This is the conclusion
Of this wonderful fusion.
Through water it emerges,
With its invisible purges,
Cleansing your channels,
Preparing new canals.
Through sunlight it blossoms,
Presenting its beauty as though it's a duty,
Expansive, soft and open,
It passes through the broken,
The lonely nights,
The many frights,
The scars of war,
Rejection and loss,
It's found the way,
It has carried its cross,
And just like the moss that splits the rock,
The hardened block,
It came through the shock.
Through the heavy, sticky mud of life,
It found a way to pass through the strife,

It trusted when most busted,
It yielded when most shielded,
It opened in its time of broken.
Through the constant showers of hardship,
It found a new partnership,
When all were running here and there,
It didn't care.
Instead it remained quietly dead,
Still without the thrills,
The constant pills,
These deep lonely chills.
The flower's simplicity and elegance,
Its quintessence is full of presence,
A sign of all times,
A reminder of how we can shine,
And come out of our crimes,
Then stepping into our prime.
Through the thick, lonely mud,
Alone, without sight,
No clear path,
Slivering and sliding through the unknown,
With no clear reference,

But only its presence,
It slowly arises,
Following the small still voice,
It yields to its choice, and touches the sun,
And as it travels deeper towards the light,
The flower in that very hour becomes its
Reflection, its warmth, its love, it's projection.
It embodies its glory,
Its communion is now its union,
The marination,
Its determination,
The path of light immersing,
The journey complete!

EARTH DAY

I hope we have Earth Day in our yearly diary to reconnect with all our neighbours, Friends and co-workers, the animals and forests, to say, "Sorry at the way we have treated you, farmed you, used you for sport, hunted you down, and treated you with such cruelty".

I am absolutely sure that if we did this consciously to animals, forests, streams and our rivers, things would heal on our planet and change for the better.

Everything is so intimately interconnected and finely tuned that I know if we did this, there would be a return to a much deeper sense of unity and compassion.

This is a repentance that needs to happen as there's just way too much cruelty on our planet.

SEMBAH

If you bow to the awakened nature of others,
You will surely see their true colours.
Not the stain and pain of your own views,
For how can you tell their journey, their shoes?
Bowing to the awakened nature of the others,
Is becoming one with all your brothers.
Please bow to the awakened nature of others,
For some have had no mothers,
No sisters, no brothers.
Bow to the awakened nature of the others
because many have had few lovers.
Rejection is a powerful projection,
it's far worse than any infection!
When you bow to the awakened nature of
others,
your love covers.
I bow to you with my head and heart.

Sembah

ALONG THE PATH

There's going to be someone you meet on your
path today or this week who will need a word
of encouragement, a gesture of kindness, a
helping hand, a warm embrace.

But then again, it might be you that needs it. If
humans can be cruel at times for no reasons,
then we can also be kind, simply because we
are all one, made from the same stuff.

For there is no greater love than to lay your life
down for a friend.

SO YOU WANT TO FLY?

So you want to expand your wings,
expand your vision, fly and coast through life
without a care in the world?
Really?
Let's start looking at the things that are
currently weighing you down,
The things that that you have become too
attached to,
The things that you are trying to control or
avoid, but are in fact the perfect lessons you
need to build your wings!
Or what about the things that you might be
gripping and clinching at,
The things that are keeping you all locked up in
the wrong places?
What about holding on to the wrong people in
your life, those that are there pulling you into
their own dramas and confusion?
What about getting distracted into areas that
are only wasting your precious time?

What about allowing the past, or past mistakes
in your life to condemn you, when in fact you
know full well that you have learnt your
lessons, and have taken full responsibility, and
that there is no past?
It doesn't exist anymore!
What about the things that you identify with as
"yourself" but in fact are just ideas,
constructs, thoughts and emotions that are
spinning around in your head?
Your true light, your true self, your true
essence, is one of courage.
It carries the exact wisdom you require.
It truly knows where to guide you and how to
guide you.
But, condition: you have to be humble and
present to hear and follow its whispers and
guidance.
Trust who you are and find your freedom.

WHOLEHEART

Wholehearted living is about engaging in our lives from a place of worthiness. It means cultivating the Courage, Compassion, and Connection to wake up in the morning and think, no matter what gets done and how much is left undone, I am enough."
Living authentically means that we understand and embrace who we are, including our faults, failures and imperfections.
We must muster the courage to own imperfection, set boundaries and allow ourselves to be vulnerable while practicing self-compassion when we fall short.
There is no connection to others without vulnerability.
Ironically, vulnerability is the first thing we look for in others, but it is the last thing we feel comfortable showing to others.

Many people view vulnerability as weakness
and it is that attitude that interferes with deep
meaningful relationships.
When we choose to cultivate authenticity while
letting go of what others think, we can
cultivate real connections in our lives.
People will see us for who we are, and we will
feel accepted instead of the shallower feeling
of "fitting in".

LIFE IS CALLING YOU DEEPER

Remember this - When the wind is blowing your
branches to and fro, your vision is blurred, the
people you called friends, walked away.
You feel like life is tearing you down and you're
alone in the desert!
Stand firm my good friend,
life is calling you deeper.
Deeper into the magic of stillness,
deeper into the wisdom and clarity of your own
unique light, where inspiration and direction,
is waiting to direct you into a new life.
It may feel like you're breaking,
and maybe you are.
It may feel as dry and as barren as the desert,
but my dear friend this is another chance for
you to touch your centre, your most powerful
part of who you are, and alone is the only way
you can do this.
Alone with the Earth, the trees, the stars, the
sky, the lakes, the rivers, the beauty of life

whispering, "I have got your back, I am there, just trust. Stand still, I am walking with you..." Like a tree, dig into the soil of stillness and watch your new branches grow.

THE NARROW PATH

Should someone slander you,
gossip or try and discredit you over mistakes
you have made.
Throughout a billion worlds,
and with a heart full of love,
proclaim his good qualities in return,
with an understanding, that he may be
suffering, bound, trapped or lacking self-love.
Love those who wrong you,
do good to those who despise you.
The narrow path is not for the faint hearted.

THE WIND

Remember that the birds of the air, the trees,
the rivers, the air we breathe are all our
neighbours, our friends, our companions on this
sacred journey we call life.
The light, the spirit of truth has no form, it is
like the wind, you feel it but cannot see it. Yet
you know it's there.
The wind blows wherever it pleases.
You hear its sound, but you cannot tell where it
comes from or where it is going.
So it is with everyone born of the Spirit.
To know the spirit is to let go of form.

IT AIN'T OVER UNTIL IT'S OVER

You have more in you than your emotions are
screaming out, than your thoughts are saying,
than your disappointments are reminding you
of, than your past fears are quenching you
with, than people's projective fears are
telling you!
You have a power, a force, a will, a focus, a
choice, a determination that is ready to rise,
ready to pounce, ready to silence all your
doubts, all your fears!
So gather your courage, take a deep breath in,
focus your heart and mind, and start walking in
the direction of where you know you should be
walking in, where your true liberty is waiting
and your truth is calling you to celebrate
with you!
It may seem a touch uncomfortable, a little
nervy but I can see your breakthrough!
Small steps forward - I hear!

Small steps in the right direction are worth
more than huge steps in the wrong direction!
I can hear it, and so can you!
Come on rise!
It may be lonely, it may even be dark and
painful but you owe it to yourself and
no one else!
And you know something, you are never alone!
Courage always attracts courage!
Rise and keep moving forward,
it ain't over until it's over!

BUTTERFLY

When the butterfly spoke to me.
"Hey my friend, cheer up. I didn't start too
elegantly, or eloquently. In fact, I began as a
tiny caterpillar, afraid to get trampled."
Crawling really slowly, up and down,
some days thinking I would even drown.
But I followed my instincts to eat leaves,
hoping that one day I would grow some wings,
so I could fly above the kings.
This was my vision and faith to transform, to
metamorphosis, to change into the beauty and
glory I felt inside...
So just because your outside world is torn and
heavy, and your circumstances tough and
rough, don't give up on who you are,
and what you see...
Even if you have to eat leaves and grip tightly
for a while, know that your time of
change will come.

Perseverance, endurance, is what I practiced,
just like my friend John the Baptist.
My next stage on this journey, we call life,
meant that I had to hang upside down on a tree
in the form of a pupa.
Another change into the strange.
So, don't be afraid of being different,
or looking silly, or hanging around trees.
Trees are special,
many a miracle happens there.
Some find life, others a wife,
while others deal with suffering.
As for me I was about to explode into beauty
and splendour, from a pupa.
Doesn't even sound cool right? You see from
the outside, it looks like nothing is happening.
That's the key, things are always happening in
stillness, this is where the magic really takes
place, under the shadow of stillness
and deep prayer.
All my parts and individual pieces are
growing and newly forming,

and I am about to grow new wings so I can
become a deep follower of the wind.
That's right, the wind.
This invisible force is going to be my new
friend, it's going to take me places that I have
always dreamed about, always longed to see
and touch.
I like to call him "the breath of all life",
the sacred one, because I can hear his
beautiful, soft voice that I have trusted, and
trusting. And soon it's going to lead me into
the deepest victory, the most beautiful sun set,
and I will finally be able to see with my new
heart, with my new vision.
I have learnt to trust and follow this small, still,
creative voice and I hope my dear friend you
will too. Please remember how I started!
I will finally have the elegance, poise and beauty
that I could feel from deep within soon, but my
dear friends, it has taken time, patience and
even long suffering.

I love you all my dear friends, and if I can do it,
You can!
Please don't give up just because it's rather
lonely, or hard, or even painful.
Please trust what you see, what you feel, what
you sense, who you are and what you can be.
The same spirit that has transformed me into
this majestic creature is living in you,
closer than your very breath. I love you dearly,
and every phase, chapter, day and detail of
your life matters to me.

YOU ARE A WONDER

The universe is filled with many wonders, with
many gifts, with many treasures, with many
magical moments, with many beautiful stories,
with many wonderful memories, with many
beautiful friends, with many surprises, with
many inspirations, and if you are reading this
now, I honestly want you to know that you, yes
you, are one of them.
Keep being you,
it's your greatest gift to all of us.

CHANGE

Time to throw the old and try something new.
Now, faith is the substance of things hoped
for, the evidence of things not seen.
Casting your nets on the wrong side,
without sensing the tide,
or feeling the ride?
Currents of change,
I know this may sound strange,
But when the wind blows,
And the Word speaks and
reveals your leaks,
It's time to throw your nets on the other side,
And try something new!
You may be gripping too tightly to the old,
Or stuck in a routine,
Or set in the past like some rigid cast.
And the wind is blowing and showing a new
way.
That's right, this very day!
But you're afraid of change,

To rearrange,
A little scared of the strange,
Of being different.
But fear not,
For when the word enters your boat,
Its creative power,
Its dynamic force will appear
as a powerful horse.
The Word is filled with light,
The very same essence
that is carrying your presence!
The visible and the invisible will suddenly align,
Just at the exact time.
This ain't no rhyme,
But a challenge to throw down your nets daily.

COSMIC FREQUENCIES

According to NASA, there are 100 billion stars
in the Milky Way alone.
Who knows, there could be more or less, but
one thing we are certain about is that the
universe is a vast ocean of wonder and
mystery.
So, remember to look up today, it's important.
It helps you to remember that you and your
problems are both infinitesimally small and that
you are a piece of an amazing and vast
universe, and every day is a miraculous part of
a journey.
I don't feel separate at all to any life.
I feel in every part of me that we are one.

"If you want to find the secrets of the
universe, think in terms of energy, frequency,
and vibrations." - Nicola Tesla

I see the universe like a vast river, a living stream that's constantly flowing, directed by currents of liquid love, in a vast musical orchestra of sound waves, that keeps everything together in something we call Law and Order.

It's something I feel very deep within me and started happening a lot more after training the Kembangan many years ago.

I don't expect anyone to believe me because it's not a belief or dogma, but rather a deep sense and living awareness within me that I see and feel.

I sense the oneness of the universe and the interconnectedness of the universe together.

We are all truly One.

It's like we are woven into a vast tapestry of threads that are totally unique, but together in this vast ocean, being the wave and the ocean at the same time.

We have our specific orders, frequencies and
laws here and once we find the correct
harmonies, we flow,
very much like beautiful music playing.
Love, compassion, kindness, humility are the
frequencies that allow us to flow with this
eternal river of love, and peace is the song that
will be sung.
This is what I feel. I see it everywhere - in the
face of a dolphin or a child, or in the sunset, or
the faces of you and me.
We are One.

KEEP MOVING FORWARD

Yes, there may be many things I can't do,
but there are also many things I can do!
I need to focus on those things and set myself
goals based on the things I can do right now,
rather than holding myself back by thinking
about all the things I'd like to do, if only...
We all need to start somewhere. Why not start
where you are right now, no matter what you
have and whatever is happening in your life?
Take that small step today, even if you're
afraid, even if you don't want to, even if your
mind tries to talk you out of it. My mind tries
to do that all the time!
You'll feel amazing once you've taken that
small step, and that wonderful feeling will help
you take the next step.
"If you can't fly then run, if you can't run then
walk, if you can't walk then crawl, but
whatever you do you have to keep moving
forward." - Martin Luther King Jr.

BECOME LIKE A CHILD

Give yourself permission...
To flop,
To drop,
To lose,
To fail,
To come last,
To make mistakes,
To get it wrong,
To slide,
To fall,
To not be sure.
Remember when you were child and your
mother placed you on the ground?
How many times did you roll over, slip, slide,
trip over, before you walked?
We are not here to be perfect,
we are here to be as we are.
Accept yourself as you are. It's a gift.
For unless you become like a child you will
never experience fullness of joy.

MOTHER EARTH

"But ask the animals, and they will teach you,
or the birds in the sky, and they will tell you; or
speak to the earth, and it will teach you, or let
the fish in the sea inform you."
- Job 12:7-10 (NIV)

Nature is calling you back into a beautiful
harmonious union, where she will reveal her
beauty and treasures.
We are all enough as we are, there's no need to
be anything else. Mother earth is sitting in a
beautiful stillness sharing her love, nutrition and
wisdom. But she also has laws and these laws
need to be respected.
You are wonderfully and beautifully made.
Today, settle in your enough-ness.
Truth shall spring out of the Earth.
The Earth speaks,
For she is a witness.
When the red and the white are revealed,

And the number ten fulfilled.
When the mark, code, number and name are
introduced through guilt and shame.
There, in the centre, a light will spring forth.
A message of love,
Sent from above.
For Blessed are the meek,
for they shall inherit the Earth.

THE DAYS OF NOAH

The name 'Noah' means "rest or repose"
A name that best describes his vibe.
For when those around were being pressed
and stressed,
Noah found grace to end the chase!
He chose to find repose.
Not worried about his clothes,
Or the latest shows,
Instead he cultivated a union,
A very deep communion,
So that one day he could have a reunion.
Noah was a soul at peace,
And day by day this was his increase.
He didn't care about the latest lease,
Or the next holiday to Greece.
Peace was his measure, his deepest treasure!
In his daily life,
those around were in huge strife,
Knife crime was on the rise,
The lies we're like poisonous flies,

The corruption was stirring eruptions,
The evil of people's hearts was tearing the
Earth apart.
The beautiful Earth,
For all it's worth,
Was filled with many being killed,
With huge parts being drilled!
Violence and greed,
A new generation and breed,
And our true image
being wasted like a toxic spillage!
So when these laws were being broken,
The soul of Noah became awoken.
He turned away from the cooperate mess,
And instead drew close to the very life that
was deeply woven in his chest.
He sat so still,
Away from the thrill,
Until his will was ready to fulfil!
The karmic law of sowing and reaping,
The fact that people were sleeping,
A wave of destruction was slowly sweeping!

The weather changes,
The storms with unusual norms,
busting through all forms.
Transforming without warning.
Earthquakes with shakes
that measured with ever increasing pressure,
Tornadoes that twist and turn,
Volcanos that burn,
Until man decides to learn!
But Noah was listening
to the signs of the times,
The posts of the past ghosts,
The shadows that were pointing
to the anointing,
And the appointing of an hour that
Was about to become very sour!
And so, Noah began to build an Ark,
This was his mark,
From the centre of his spark.
His sign,
The new shrine,
A home,

A new abode,
He showed,
For those who could read the code!
The years went past,
And Noah continued to fast,
Warning people there was
coming a blast,
"A flood is coming,
The earth is humming,
I hear the drumming,
The sound is all around,
Awaken and put down your bacon,
I am not mistaken,
Please don't be forsaken,
There is coming a flood,
It's no respecter of your blood,
Your colour, your creed,
Your internal greed,
Please take heed,
And read with speed!
There's coming an hour
that will wipe out every tower,

The universal laws that are being
transgressed,
This will only lead to further unrest.
These laws have no claws,
If we transgress,
we end up in a mess,
This ain't no game of chess.
The All placed them,
For the All,
Not our fall.
Every creature,
Every tree,
Every flee,
You and me!"
So to conclude,
'Noah' means to rest.
This is a state of blessed,
So stop the chasing,
And pop the racing,
Find your stillness.
Your home,
Your Ark,

Your true spark,
A true abode,
And rest In Peace!

YOU ARE ENOUGH

Enough in the world for everyone's need,
but not enough for everyone's greed.
Enough to enjoy and be content,
Enough to prevent us from killing for
a single cent.
Enough to settle and find a space
for the whole entire human race.
Enough to share our wealth,
So that all can enjoy national health.
Enough to walk peacefully,
Respecting each and every soul equally.
Enough to feed every mouth
from here to the deep South.
Enough to shelter and home,
From the least to those who live in Rome.
You are enough!
Let no one tell you different,
That you are not insignificant.
You are perfectly and wonderfully
loved as you are,

A true shining star.
Your light and life is precious,
You're a sacred moment in time,
Yet to reach your prime.
So climb to your rightful place,
And keep that space,
To shine your original face.
You are enough.

HOME

I was crushed and found my home,
I was buried and found my light,
I was empty and yet I was filled.
I was filled and yet I was empty,
I was alone, and yet I was with the All.
I was bruised, battered, open, vulnerable, lost,
weak, scattered, torn, and yet somehow,
I found my home.
It was calling me back,
It was whispering and yet I could not hear,
My heart had hardened,
My eyes became dim,
My heart became heavy,
I was weary,
I was tired,
And yet I returned home.

HIGHWAY OF LOVE

The flower that is crushed still sends
a sweet-smelling aroma.
A forgiving heart that is crushed
does the same.
Even in its pain,
it finds room to send a sweet-smelling aroma.
For forgiveness is birthed
out of love and love covers all,
In it there is nothing other than its essence.
Love does not dishonour others,
It is not self-seeking,
It is not easily angered,
It keeps no record of wrongs.
This is the way of all ways,
The highway of Love.

HIGHEST THOUGHTS

Keep your highest thoughts, your dreams, your
aspirations, your most sacred intentions alive
and close to your heart always.
They are sacred to you, special, so don't let
anything rob them from you, or dampen them.
They are in your precious heart for you to
follow them.

BE YOURSELF

Don't hide your magic,
Don't hide your creativity,
Don't hide your colours,
Don't hide your mistakes,
Don't hide your opinions,
Don't hide the way you see things, even if you
are the only one standing.
Be yourself!
It's your gift to us all and part of your journey.
You were never called to be perfect,
you were called to be you.

YOUR FIRST AND YOUR LAST

The problem is you think you have time.
Live as though it's your last day,
Eat as though it's your first and last meal.
Train as though it's your first and last time.
Walk in the park as though you are saying your
last goodbye.
Every day is a precious moment.
This way you will have no regrets.
Read this as though it's your first time reading
and your last.
We are creating the conditions
in and around us.
By living in the way, you will live with no
regrets.

A CHILD'S HEART

A child's heart,
Playfully open,
Full of emotion,
Its devotion,
as vast as the ocean.
Searching to discover and play,
The truest magic of all our days.
A vast and wild imagination,
Without any blemish or discrimination.
Nor distinction or separation.
Able to bend and flow
as though life is one big show.
A child's heart is always ready to impart
its true colours to others,
Especially their mothers.
They slip, and fall, they slide,
But without the pride.
They are quick to say "sorry",
And fix their mistakes,
And shortly after ready to embrace.

They are soft and caring,
Living in the now,
With no concerns about money,
Or being cool,
And always ready to look the fool.
No limits to their imagination,
And always creating in every situation.
They play with anything and everyone,
And what they live for
is simply to have fun.
No boundaries,
No gates,
Everyone's a potential mate.
Curious with questions,
And plenty of suggestions.
Discovering this and that,
And always ready to have a chat.
Remember you were once this child,
Full of laughter and adventure.

REMEMBER

Remember when you were young and free,
light without care, without the worries and
cares of the world?
Remember when you could play the whole day
with simple things like paper, stones, conkers,
and spend the whole day climbing trees?
When your imagination ran wild, with abundant
energy and you slept without a care.
That playful nature is still there, that
imagination is still there, that simplicity is still
there. It's the same life, with different
circumstances and a few years older.
But that same spark who wants to laugh,
giggle, wiggle, play, explore and let its hair
down is still there,
that's of course if you still have hair ;)
Either way it's time for you to wiggle, and
giggle again. A time to recapture that magic
and innocence again. A time to gaze into the
night sky and evoke those dreams, those

adventures. I know it's been a hard and testing at times, but your spirit is bigger, and your dreams are worth exploring fully.

Just because our circumstances have not been conducive, it doesn't mean that our hearts, our dreams, our vision, need to be trashed.

Unite with that child, that wild spark within you, get up, dust yourself off and keep moving forward.

Everything changes and comes to an end.

Prepare and look up to the stars from where your strength comes from.

HEAR HER CALLING

Come, let's walk into the dimension of less talk.
The sacred path, the narrow road,
through the gate and into a clean slate.
Where there's no judgment, or pulling down,
in fact, you will feel your true crown.
Nature's calling but are you walking?
Her healing voice, it's entirely your choice,
her quiet whisper, her gentle ways are here to
enhance such wonderful days.
She's calling, "Come out of your mourning"
The moment of spring where nature opens
its magic ring.
Cures, remedies, herbs, flowers and
special plants, so please take a glance.
Explore her tour, the water so pure.
The smells, the shells, the hidden wells.
She's calling in case you're falling.
Her special embrace to the entire human race,
this sacred space where you enter grace.
She's calling, she's talking,

but the question is, are you walking?
Alone, you enter her thrown,
as you are,
no need to change,
she's waiting for a unique exchange.
Nature is whispering but are you listening?
"Come and walk, let's talk,
for we are friends, until the end.
Let's share, for I care,
you plant and I produce your food,
your shelter, your herbs, your taste,
and always with love and never with haste."

A NEW WAY

Just because you don't agree on things,
see things the same way,
believe the same things,
think the same way,
doesn't mean he's wrong.
There's no need to fight or argue.
Rather, accept the differences and
keep moving forward.
Maybe you have come to a new point,
and life is teaching you a new way of
dealing with things.

DUALITY

Duality is not a reality,
It's only a belief that offers temporary relief.
Let me explain,
I hope it's not in vain.
For in truth, duality will only distort your reality.
For anytime you split, divide or oppose,
You create a rule and a destructive tool.
Separation only leads a generation
into high and low,
In and out,
Clean and dirty,
Winner and loser,
And now guess who's a boozer?
With far more accusers!
This makes it easier
to rule and conquer,
Divide and collide,
And spin humanity
on a false ride.
Good vs evil,

The rich and the poor,
The black and the white,
A dangerous fight.
The right and the left,
Left and the right,
This duality will soon become your reality,
I told you it's insanity.
Good and bad and bad and good,
That's the reason we have the hood.
A belief in two powers will create the
experience of two forces,
Running against each other
like two wild horses.
When in fact, voice and tone
work perfectly together
to aid your phone.
You see,
first and last follow each other,
Racing and chasing,
Both end up pacing.
Life, energy, space and time,
Blending together,

No different to the weather.
Hot, cold, misty or rainy,
An atmosphere of seasons for every year.
But, in fact, they are all One,
Under our Sun.
All required and authentically inspired.
So, in the dimension of duality,
We create a false reality.
A winner becomes a loser,
A loser a winner,
Fat becomes thin,
Are you seeing this destructive spin?
These concepts, beliefs and ideas
are only forming notions of isolation,
Not supporting your true liberation.
That's why we have the poor and the rich,
The clean and the bitch,
The slave and the free,
And that's not life
for you and me.
We are all light, bright energy,
Working together in a cosmic synergy.

Sound-wave and particle,
But let's go further into this article.
The political scene in the US has been
a clear game of chess.
To be perfectly honest,
A huge mess.
The rise of Donald Trump
has given a lot of people the hump.
This current division needs some revision.
Both sides spinning their wheel,
Not keeping it real.
And now the elections
have revealed their infections.
Black vs white,
Blue vs red,
Too many lives,
And so many dead!
We are one expression of life,
Breathing and being,
Sharing the same Sun,
The same Earth,
From here to Perth!

Briefs and ideas
should not replace
our living space.
We are one race,
Within one space.
Elections should be an honest
reflection of the people's projections.
May this divide no longer collide.
We are one mind,
Universal,
And Eternal.

REAL MAGIC

When we were children, we could sit and
play with lego, leaves, stones, or with each
other and only the present existed.
We could play for hours and our parents
would trust that all is well.
Time flew by as we were all taken by the magic
and laughter of this energy that adults called
'life' and we called 'fun'.
There were no judgmental barriers,
no walls of division, no colour, no religious
dogmatic differences, no upper class, or
working class, no political divides.
It was a wonderful flow of time and space and
we didn't care what it was labelled as long as
it was fun.
We had simple things to play with, sometimes
made of paper, stones, marbles or just by
ourselves with our wild imagination.
We could sit for hours, without any sitting
practice.

We were in the magic of the moment,
without books, guides and quotes everywhere.
Or supplements, or special protein formulas.
Our energy was endless, our hearts wide and
all we wanted was to enjoy the moment with
our friends and family.
And that was the real magic!
So where has that bright open spark, that
playful soul disappeared to?
Is she or he hiding or buried somewhere, or too
bruised and tired of the playground they have
experienced outside?
It's a highly competitive, cruel world out there,
where people have lost their souls in the pursuit
of survival.
So, build your own playground,
just like you did when you were kid.
When the same stuff was spinning in the heads
of the people we called adults.
You don't need to play in their playground.
In fact, it's totally boring!

So, what would happen if you decided to just have fun, to stop caring so much about this or that, and not having more, or not being enough, or trying harder, or being right or wrong all the time?

Isn't life too short and precious to be wasting our time and energy on squabbles and useless, endless games that are not enjoyable?

The real magic is here with us whispering, "Return to zero, let go again and play, laugh, enjoy, stop caring so much, let's watch the night sky, and play in the snow, run in the forest, climb some trees, laugh again. Let your hair down a little, because in a blink of an eye it suddenly all changes."

ORIGINS

Nature is sitting with you,
To be still with the All,
To stand tall.
Still feel small?
Life's wonderful expressions,
All part of the many lessons,
Sweet and sour,
All part of the hour.
Cold yet dry,
It's ok to cry,
To let go,
To give up the grip,
And find the naked strip.
To inhale, to exhale,
The male and the female.
Our, not mine,
Thy, not I,
We, and not me,
The essence of free.
A calling to return,

To original face,
Your sacred space,
The end of the race.
Competition dies,
The real you, flies.
No more left and right,
A struggle, a fight!
It's all life expression,
It works by its own progression.
Zero interference,
No need for your perseverance.
There's harmony and health,
There's synergy with this mystical energy.
There's space and total acceptance.
Natures embrace,
Observe, it's not in the race.

SPIRIT AND LIGHT

We are spirit and light.
What this means is that we're designed
for any fight.
So let me explain,
As there's no need for fright.
The current challenge is an opportunity
for you to grow and strengthen your
entire immunity,
For yourself and your community.
How?
Quit the booze and put on your dancing shoes.
Eat when you're hungry,
But stay away from the junky.
Calm your mind by doing things to unwind.
Plenty of laughter and good sleep thereafter.
Wash your hands and take a stroll on
the sands.
Fruits, vegetables and lentils
and a regular check for the dentals.
Follow the rules but don't be a fool.

We are spirit and light,
Energy with a mysterious chemistry.
A biology that is linked to the cosmology,
The ecology, and with a chronology.
You have history, a present and future.
You are not alone.
Your body is both energy and matter,
Powered by an eternal battery.
This is no flattery.
We have the power to transform energy
into chemical, water, carbon,
Minerals and oxygen,
Rich organic compounds,
Right here and now, on these grounds.
A photosynthesis of epic proportions,
Working perfectly without distortions.
You are a light worker,
And energy transformer,
A true reformer!
And this energy never dies,
So please don't believe the lies.

Fact: you can check it before it gets censored,
tracked, or controlled,
as the great seers foretold.
The Law of thermodynamics:
energy cannot be created, nor destroyed!
So quit playing God,
And telling us we are void!
We're alive,
We exchange,
We give and receive,
We conceive,
We perceive,
We often grieve,
So, you better believe,
There's no retrieve!
We are not digital or a number,
Away with easy slumber.
We are not data called to live in beta!
We are not robots,
Or machines that have been designed
and controlled just to grind.
Again, fact!

And no matter of whether we believe or not,
We are writing our own headlines,
Our own news,
That's called "walking in your own shoes!"
Your light, your spirit
will echo throughout space and time, eternally.
And this, my friends, is the truth,
And how it ends.

STARS

"I address you all tonight as true stars, my wonderful brothers and sisters. Completely dazzling in your sacred uniqueness, unlike any other in the entire universe.

In fact, without you, I would never have known the possibilities that your courage has shown me, that your love has shown me, that your perseverance has shown me.

I want to thank you for being you and showing us all that we are here to be different and yet work together".

YOU

Your greatest gift to us all is YOU.
You being you is the greatest gift.
You being you is essential in releasing your
uniqueness.
So, never stop being you!
That's your gift to you and everyone.
Never stop being you,
Because that's who you are.
It's you!

TIME TO RISE

This is a time for all of us to work and walk
together with cords of love and unity.
It's a time to find your inner freedom.
And when you do, be a strength and light to
others. It's a time to share your love and not
hold back because others are locked in or
locked up.
It's a time to expand your vision and breath
hope into your dreams.
It's a time to gallop into the direction of what
you cherish and value.
It's time for you to shine.
Rise up and be the best you can.
Rise up and shine.
Rise up and do your best training,
or cooking, or cleaning, or work.
Rise up and be the best friend, the best father,
the best mother, the best mentor.
Rise up and walk side by side with those you
love. Until the last breath.

MOVE SLOWLY

Remember to walk slowly,
Eat slowly,
Drive slowly,
Work calmly.
You are the very thing you are seeking.
Therefore, be extra kind to yourself.
Train as though you are floating in
the Universe,
Allowing the it breathes you to guide your
motion, movement, speech and action.
We are all children in the universe.
Enjoy and play with loving hearts.

YOU ARE ENOUGH

You can bend for people and they will say,
"You're not bendy enough", or lay down and
they will say, "You're not straight enough", or
stand up and they will scream, "You're not tall
enough". Our planet is filled with a disease
called "You're not enough as you are". You're
not rich enough, white enough, tall enough, fat
enough, ripped enough, clever enough, and the
list continues in every direction and in
every way!
You're a kid growing up with all the other
pressures of life pressing on you and now
you're told "You're not quite enough as
you are."
Well, here's where you need to listen:
You're the only person on the Earth that is
You. Therefore, you are a creation of
uniqueness, an authentic, majestic, wonderful
miracle of life expressed and lived through your
own unique character, vision and insight.

Enough of not feeling enough! There's no one
quite like you, there's no need to try either and
be different, fit in, or work at anything.
Only be yourself, for yourself!
The moment you sense your uniqueness,
is the moment you will feel an acceptance and
a deep appreciation of who you are, and
then you're home.
You're really home!
Because no one will ever be able to make you
feel inadequate, small, worthless, useless, or
not-enough again! You wake up every day
feeling, I was born to be me, and me is who I
shall be. Take it or leave it but this this is
Who I Am!
WOW! What a freedom, what peace, what joy!
Now go and be yourself and know that
yourself, is always enough!

Let the end be the beginning...

Printed in Great Britain
by Amazon